Dinosaurs

Rachel Firth

Designed by Neil Francis,
Nickey Butler & Cecilia Bonilla

Illustrated by Franco Tempesta & John Woodcock
Scientific consultants: Dr. David Martill & Darren Naish

A Styracosaurus

Contents

Internet links

For links to the websites recommended in this book, go to the **Usborne Quicklinks Website** at www.usborne-quicklinks.com and enter the keywords "discovery dinosaurs". Usborne Publishing is not responsible for the content on any website other than its own. Please read the Internet safety guidelines on the Usborne Quicklinks Website and on page 62 of this book.

★ Pictures in this book with a star symbol beside them can be downloaded for your own personal use from the Usborne Quicklinks Website.

What are dinosaurs?

Dinosaurs belonged to a group of animals called reptiles. They lived between 240 and 65 million years ago, long before people existed, in a time called the Mesozoic era. All animals that lived before people are called prehistoric animals.

Different dinosaurs

There were many different kinds of dinosaurs, although they didn't all live at the same time as each other. Some were very big and others were small. Many were fast, but some were slow. However, they all lived on dry land and none could fly.

Prehistoric animals

While dinosaurs lived on land, flying reptiles filled the skies and huge reptiles lived in the oceans. Other animals still living today, such as crocodiles and sharks, also lived at the same time as the dinosaurs.

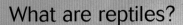

What are reptiles?

Reptiles are animals, such as snakes, crocodiles and turtles, that have scaly, waterproof skin. Most reptiles have legs that stick out sideways from their bodies. But dinosaurs had legs that supported their bodies from underneath. This meant that smaller dinosaurs could run faster than other reptiles. Dinosaur legs were also stronger than other reptiles' legs.

Like other reptiles, this green tree python has scaly skin.

The shape of a lizard's legs stops it from running fast for very long.

Without such strong legs, a very heavy Triceratops dinosaur wouldn't be able to stand up.

Changing world

Dinosaurs lived on Earth for millions of years. Being faster and bigger helped them to be so successful. But they also survived for so long because they were able to adapt, or change. During the Mesozoic era, there were dramatic changes in the weather and even the shape of the land. Not all types of animals were able to survive these changes as dinosaurs did.

This is a Stegosaurus, a dinosaur that lived about 145–150 million years ago.

 Internet links

For links to websites where you can find lots of dinosaur activities, games and quizzes and explore a dinosaur family tree, go to **www.usborne-quicklinks.com**

Fact: More than ten previously unknown dinosaurs are discovered every year.

5

Fantastic fossils

Amazingly, even though dinosaurs died out millions of years ago, we can still find out much about them. Like many other plants and animals, some dinosaurs were preserved as fossils. By studying their fossils, we can piece together a picture of what they were like.

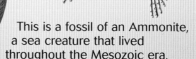

This is the fossil skeleton of a Seymouria. It was fossilized about 250 million years ago.

This is a fossil of an Ammonite, a sea creature that lived throughout the Mesozoic era.

Becoming a fossil

A fossil usually starts to form when a dead animal is buried in sand or mud, called sediment. Over millions of years, more and more sediment builds up in layers, and slowly turns to stone.

Chemicals, or minerals, in the stone seep down into tiny holes in the bones and teeth of the animal. The chemicals very gradually become hard, and the animal skeleton becomes a fossil.

Fact: Scientists can guess how fast a dinosaur moved by looking at the gaps between its footprints.

Stony bones

Fossils of hard things, like bone and teeth, are called body fossils. We can use them to estimate how big dinosaurs were and what shape they were. People who study fossils are called paleontologists.

The bones of this fossilized dinosaur are heavier than ordinary bones because they have hardened chemicals inside them.

 Internet links

For links to websites where you can watch animations of how fossils form and find out how to collect fossils, go to **www.usborne-quicklinks.com**

Rare finds

Very rarely, the soft parts of animals, such as muscles and kidneys, are fossilized too. Fossils like these are so rare because soft parts usually decay before they can be fossilized. They are very exciting as they can tell us about the animal's insides.

This scientist is carefully uncovering fossilized dinosaur footprints.

Fossilizing footprints

As well as fossils of bones and teeth, scientists have found fossilized animal footprints, leaves with insect bite marks in them, and even dinosaur dung. These fossils are called trace fossils.

Trace fossils are formed in slightly different ways from body fossils. For example, fossil footprints may be formed when a fresh print becomes filled with sediment. Eventually, the sediment turns to stone, preserving the shape of the footprint.

Dinosaur detectives

Dinosaur fossils are being found all the time all over the world. Sometimes they are found by chance, but usually paleontologists have a good idea about where to look for them.

Where to look

To find dinosaur fossils, paleontologists must look in the right kind of rock. Dinosaur fossils are found only in sedimentary rock that was formed during the Mesozoic era.

Promising finds

Not all sedimentary rock formed during the Mesozoic era has fossils in it. So, before they start to dig, paleontologists look for tiny pieces of dinosaur fossils on the ground. If there are pieces of bone on the surface, it's more likely that there are more bones under the ground.

Paleontologists chip away at the rock, revealing a spectacular fossilized dinosaur skeleton.

Internet links

For links to websites where you can dig up dinosaurs, examine real dinosaur fossils and reconstruct an animal skeleton online, go to **www.usborne-quicklinks.com**

Fact: The people of ancient China thought that dinosaur fossils were the teeth of dragons and ground them up to use in their medicines.

Digging up dinosaurs

Getting fossils out of rock isn't always easy. Fossils are often fragile and it can take paleontologists weeks, or even years, to free a fossil. They use all kinds of tools to help them, such as chemicals, pickaxes and even dentists' drills.

The rock around a fossil is carefully chipped away by paleontologists. Any dust on the fossil can be removed with a brush.

Once removed from the ground, fossils are wrapped in paper and covered with plaster. This hardens to protect the fossil.

Changing views

Putting dinosaur bones back together is a little like doing a jigsaw puzzle. Even with a lot of bones, it isn't always clear how the dinosaur should be rebuilt. Sometimes, scientists change their minds about how a dinosaur should look, and the dinosaur skeletons in museums have to be altered or rebuilt.

Rebuilding dinosaurs

If a lot of fossilized bones belonging to one dinosaur are found, paleontologists can try to put them back together. This helps them to see what the dinosaur looked like. If they can't find all the bones, they can often guess what the missing pieces looked like and make replacements for them.

Scientists have found enough bones to rebuild the skeleton of this Lufengosaurus.

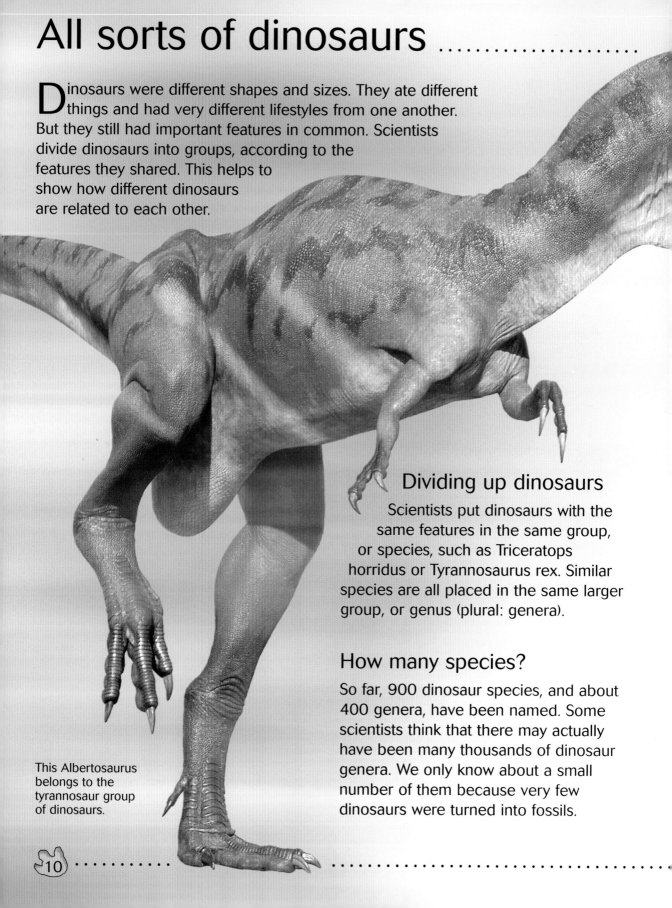

All sorts of dinosaurs ....

Dinosaurs were different shapes and sizes. They ate different things and had very different lifestyles from one another. But they still had important features in common. Scientists divide dinosaurs into groups, according to the features they shared. This helps to show how different dinosaurs are related to each other.

Dividing up dinosaurs

Scientists put dinosaurs with the same features in the same group, or species, such as Triceratops horridus or Tyrannosaurus rex. Similar species are all placed in the same larger group, or genus (plural: genera).

How many species?

So far, 900 dinosaur species, and about 400 genera, have been named. Some scientists think that there may actually have been many thousands of dinosaur genera. We only know about a small number of them because very few dinosaurs were turned into fossils.

This Albertosaurus belongs to the tyrannosaur group of dinosaurs.

Naming dinosaurs

When a new species of dinosaur is discovered, scientists make up a name for that species. The name is usually in Latin or Greek. Some dinosaur names describe the dinosaur. For example, Triceratops means "three-horned face". Other dinosaurs are named after people or places. For example, Masiakasaurus knopfleri was named after the rock singer Mark Knopfler.

Lizard hips and bird hips

Scientists divide all dinosaurs into two big groups according to the shape of their hipbones. They are called lizard-hipped, or saurischian, dinosaurs and bird-hipped, or ornithischian, dinosaurs. Modern birds have hipbones that look like those of bird-hipped dinosaurs. But surprisingly, they are in fact descended from lizard-hipped dinosaurs. Many paleontologists regard birds as living dinosaurs and call them "avian dinosaurs".

The horns above this Triceratops' eyes are about 1m (3ft) long.

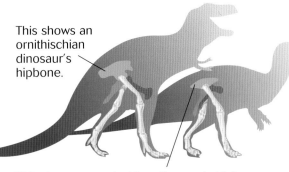

This shows an ornithischian dinosaur's hipbone.

This shows a saurischian dinosaur's hipbone.

Internet links

For links to websites where you can browse an A to Z guide to dinosaurs and play a quiz game on how dinosaurs get their names, go to **www.usborne-quicklinks.com**

Fact: The word "dinosaur" means "terrible lizard".

Big and small

When people think of dinosaurs, they often think of enormous animals. Some were amazingly big – the biggest animals ever to walk the Earth. But others were only the size of small dogs.

Amazingly long

The biggest dinosaur bone found so far belonged to Amphicoelias fragillimus. Paleontologists don't have the whole skeleton, so they have to use this bone to guess how big this dinosaur was. Some think it was as long as 60m (200ft).

Here you can see how large some of the bigger dinosaurs were compared to one of the smallest, and a human.

Brachiosaurus

Supersaurus

Compsognathus

Human

Fact: Brachiosaurus weighed about the same as 12 elephants.

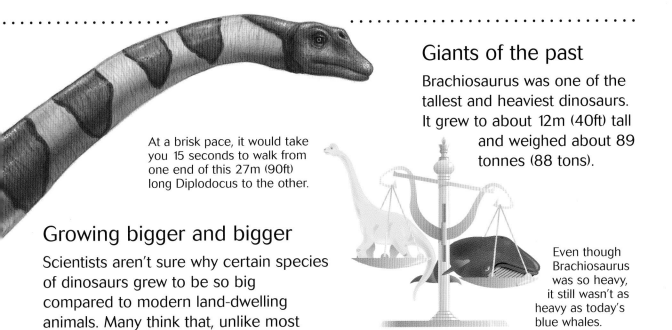

At a brisk pace, it would take you 15 seconds to walk from one end of this 27m (90ft) long Diplodocus to the other.

Giants of the past

Brachiosaurus was one of the tallest and heaviest dinosaurs. It grew to about 12m (40ft) tall and weighed about 89 tonnes (88 tons).

Even though Brachiosaurus was so heavy, it still wasn't as heavy as today's blue whales.

Growing bigger and bigger

Scientists aren't sure why certain species of dinosaurs grew to be so big compared to modern land-dwelling animals. Many think that, unlike most animals, some dinosaurs simply didn't stop growing once they became adults.

Ⓕ Internet links

For links to websites where you can read about the longest, tallest and smallest dinosaurs, and print out dinosaur size charts, go to **www.usborne-quicklinks.com**

Little dinosaurs

Fossils of small dinosaurs are very rare, so scientists aren't sure how many small dinosaurs there were. Compsognathus was one of the smallest. It was about 60cm (2ft) long and was a fast-running hunter. But the smallest dinosaur fossil found so far is the fossil of tiny dromaeosaur Microraptor. It was about 48cm (19in) long and lived in China.

Although Compsognathus was one of the smallest dinosaurs, it could run much faster than huge dinosaurs, such as Brachiosaurus.

Dinosaur bones ....

It's amazing what we can learn from dinosaur bones. They tell us much more about dinosaurs than just what shape and size they were. We can find out about their different lifestyles and even what illnesses and injuries they suffered from.

Lightening the load

Many dinosaurs, such as theropods and some of the bigger sauropods, had pockets of air, called air sacs, in their bones. These made the dinosaurs light for their size. Lighter dinosaurs were able to move much more quickly than heavier ones.

This is the skeleton of a carnivorous Gasosaurus.

Here you can see that Dryosaurus' bones were hollow, making the animal light enough to run fast.

Painful joints

The fossil of one Tyrannosaurus rex shows that it suffered from gout. Gout is a disease that can be brought on by eating too much red meat. It makes joints very swollen and painful. It seems that many dinosaurs had painful bone diseases, such as gout and arthritis.

  Fact: By studying chemicals inside dinosaur bones, paleontologists can estimate the temperature of dinosaurs' blood.

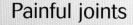

Broken bones

The biggest, best-preserved Tyrannosaurus rex skeleton belongs to a dinosaur nicknamed "Sue". Sue was named after Sue Hendrickson, who discovered her. By looking at Sue's bones, paleontologists can piece together information about her life. Sue had broken both her hind legs but, incredibly, they healed themselves while she was still alive. She may have been injured while fighting.

Under the microscope

Scientists can cut slices from dinosaurs' bones that are so thin you can see through them when they are held in front of a light. When a slice is placed under a microscope, scientists can examine the structure of the bone.

A very thin slice of dinosaur bone seen through a microscope

Food and eating

inosaurs left a lot of clues behind about the types of food they ate. Most were either carnivores (meat-eaters) or herbivores (plant-eaters). But some were omnivores (ate both meat and plants).

Fossilized food

Very rarely, paleontologists have found a dinosaur's last meal fossilized in its stomach. They have also found fossilized dung, with bits of food still inside it. These rare finds tell us exactly what dinosaurs ate.

Telling teeth

Dinosaurs had teeth that were adapted to help them eat particular types of food. By examining the shape and size of a dinosaur's teeth, scientists can guess what sort of food it liked to eat.

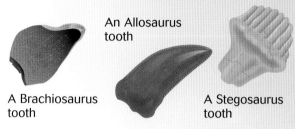

An Allosaurus tooth

A Brachiosaurus tooth

A Stegosaurus tooth

Deadly spikes

To pierce and tear the flesh off its victims, Allosaurus had very sharp knife-shaped teeth. Another carnivore, Tyrannosaurus rex, had huge, ferocious teeth, strong enough to puncture and crush bone.

Some meat-eating dinosaurs, such as these Deinonychus, use their claws as well as their teeth to rip flesh off their victims.

Fact: Dinosaur teeth fell out when they were worn, and were replaced by new ones. Sometimes dinosaurs would swallow the old teeth by mistake.

Fishing for dinner

Spinosaurs had pointed teeth, which they might have used to catch fish. They probably didn't just eat fish though. As well as fish scales, the fossilized bones of a baby Iguanodon have been found in spinosaur Baryonyx's stomach.

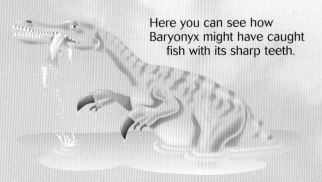
Here you can see how Baryonyx might have caught fish with its sharp teeth.

 Internet links

For links to websites where you can find games and quizzes about what dinosaurs ate and the clues left behind in fossilized dung, go to **www.usborne-quicklinks.com**

Toothless!

Not all dinosaurs had teeth. Bird-like oviraptorosaurs, such as Oviraptor, had toothless beaks shaped like the beaks of parrots. Scientists aren't sure what they ate. But the heads of little troodontid dinosaurs have been found in an Oviraptor's nest, so they may have eaten meat.

Pencils and spoons

The teeth of plant-eating dinosaurs didn't need to be razor sharp. Diplodocus had pencil-shaped teeth to pull and snip at plants. Brachiosaurus had spoon-shaped teeth to tear mouthfuls of leaves off bushes.

In spite of its ferocious appearance, this Styracosaurus is in fact a plant-eating dinosaur. It grinds down food with its sharp, beak-like mouth.

Hungry herbivores

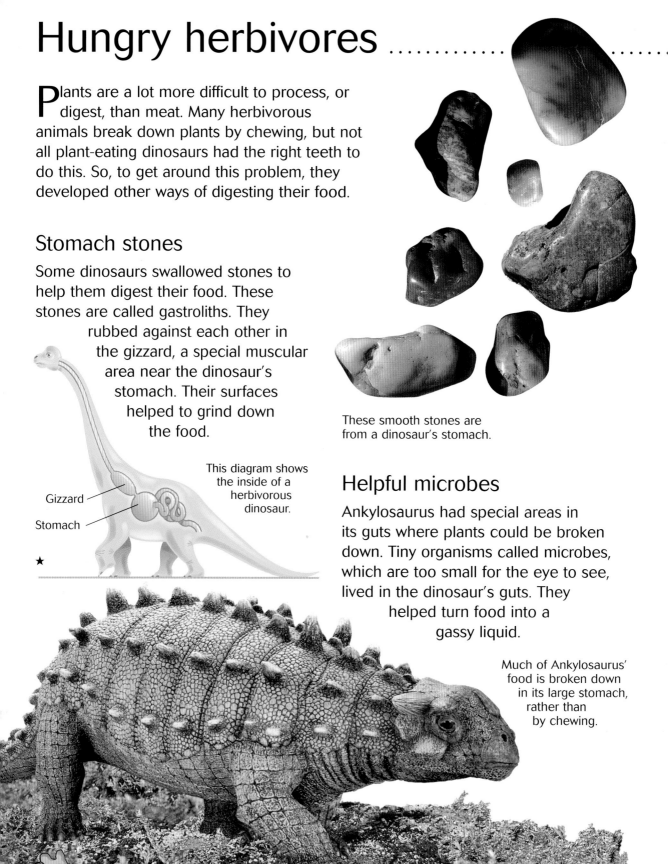

Plants are a lot more difficult to process, or digest, than meat. Many herbivorous animals break down plants by chewing, but not all plant-eating dinosaurs had the right teeth to do this. So, to get around this problem, they developed other ways of digesting their food.

Stomach stones

Some dinosaurs swallowed stones to help them digest their food. These stones are called gastroliths. They rubbed against each other in the gizzard, a special muscular area near the dinosaur's stomach. Their surfaces helped to grind down the food.

These smooth stones are from a dinosaur's stomach.

This diagram shows the inside of a herbivorous dinosaur.

Gizzard

Stomach

★

Helpful microbes

Ankylosaurus had special areas in its guts where plants could be broken down. Tiny organisms called microbes, which are too small for the eye to see, lived in the dinosaur's guts. They helped turn food into a gassy liquid.

Much of Ankylosaurus' food is broken down in its large stomach, rather than by chewing.

Grating and grinding

Hadrosaurs had two or three rows of teeth at the backs of their jaws, but none at the front. They could rub their teeth together in different directions to grind and grate their food. Hadrosaurs had as many as 2,000 teeth at any one time.

★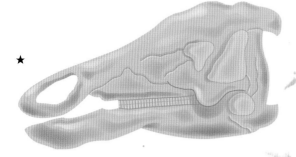

This is a picture of a hadrosaur skull showing its grinding teeth still preserved at the back of its jaws.

Big eaters

All food contains something called protein which helps animals to grow and stay healthy. Most plants have less protein in them than meat does. This meant that herbivorous dinosaurs had to eat more and spend more time eating than carnivores of the same size.

This Apatosaurus is tall enough to reach juicy new leaves on the tops of trees. They swallow them whole because their teeth aren't the right shape to chew them.

 Fact: The only known example of the giant sauropod Seismosaurus appears to have choked to death on a stone it was trying to swallow to use as a gastrolith.

Carnivorous killers ....

The only carnivorous dinosaurs were a group called theropods. They made up about a third of all dinosaurs. Animals that hunt other animals for food are known as predators, and the creatures they hunt are called prey.

On the attack

Large theropods could use their sheer size, together with deadly teeth, strong jaws and sharp claws, to overcome almost any animal. Smaller theropods would have relied more on speed and needle-sharp claws to catch and kill their prey.

This Velociraptor is hunting for prey. It's a fast runner and can overtake most other dinosaurs.

Saving energy

Although they were skilful hunters, very big theropods, such as Tyrannosaurus rex, probably scavenged if they could, eating animals that had already died. This saved them the effort of chasing after their prey.

Fact: Tyrannosaurus rex could eat as much as 230kg (500lb) of meat and bones in one mouthful. That's about the same weight as two large pigs.

Going in for the kill

Allosaurus was another large theropod. It probably attacked by taking several huge bites from its prey. It might then have left the victim for a while, waiting for it to become weak through blood loss and shock. When the prey was too weak to struggle, Allosaurus could go in for the kill.

Deadly Deinonychus

Deinonychus were only 2m (6ft) long, but they were terrifyingly efficient killers. They may have hunted in groups called packs. This would have allowed them to hunt down dinosaurs that were too big for one Deinonychus to tackle on its own.

Ⓕ Internet links

For links to websites to play dinosaur games, go to www.usborne-quicklinks.com

Here you can see how Deinonychus might have leapt onto their prey, digging their claws deep into it to kill it.

They would have slashed at their victim with sharp, half-moon shaped claws.

★

Defending themselves...............

Dinosaurs needed to protect themselves, not just from predators, but from other dinosaurs competing to live in the same place or for the same mate. Some of them had special body parts to defend themselves.

When they stop fighting, it's quite likely that the Ankylosaurus, on the right, will have fewer wounds than the Tyrannosaurus rex, on the left.

Terrible tails

Some dinosaurs could use their tails as deadly weapons. Ankylosaurus had tails with huge, heavy club-like ends. One swing from one of these might have been fatal — even to a Tyrannosaurus rex. Stegosaurus had massive 1m (3ft) long spikes on the ends of their tails, making an angry Stegosaurus very dangerous.

This fossilized tail-club of ankylosaur Euoplocephalus is 60cm (2ft) across. It was heavy enough to shatter bone.

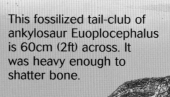

Horns and frills

Many dinosaurs had ferocious looking horns. Some dinosaurs, such as Triceratops, had huge, bony frills around their necks as well. These protected their necks. Horns and frills made dinosaurs look aggressive and were probably used to scare off enemies before fighting broke out.

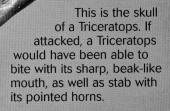

This is the skull of a Triceratops. If attacked, a Triceratops would have been able to bite with its sharp, beak-like mouth, as well as stab with its pointed horns.

Ankylosaurus' spikes and plates are embedded in protective, thick, leathery skin.

Hard heads

The top of Pachycephalosaurus' skull was 25cm (10in) thick. Some scientists think that it used it to butt its enemies' heads. Others think that, although the bone was thick, it was too fragile for this. They suggest that they may have butted their enemies' bodies with them instead.

Bony bits

Some dinosaurs had very hard bony plates covering their bodies. These protected them from the sharp teeth and claws of attackers. Ankylosaurs had bony spikes as well as bony plates, and even their eyelids were made of bone.

Pachycephalosaurus probably used its head to butt its enemies.

For a link to a website to make 3-D models of these dinosaurs, go to **www.usborne-quicklinks.com**

Slow and stupid? ....

Animals with brains that are small compared to their body size are often less intelligent than bigger-brained ones. So, some people think dinosaurs were slow and stupid because they had small brains. Some dinosaurs probably weren't very clever, but not all were stupid.

Small brain, big body

Plant-eater Apatosaurus had one of the smallest brains for its body size. Its body was about 100,000 times bigger than its brain. Many plant-eating dinosaurs had small brains, like Apatosaurus did, but this didn't matter. They spent most of their time eating plants which meant that they didn't need big, powerful brains.

The brain of this Apatosaurus is about the same size as a modern cat's brain, although its body is thousands of times bigger than a cat's body.

For a link to a website where you can take a look at Troodon, go to www.usborne-quicklinks.com

Bigger brains

Hadrosaurs had bigger brains than other plant-eating dinosaurs and were probably much more intelligent. They also had more complex lives. They lived in large groups, or herds, and scientists think that they communicated with each other by making sounds.

This shows how big a hadrosaur's brain is relative to its head.

Two brains?

Scientists once thought that sauropods and stegosaurs had second brains in their backbones. In fact, it was probably a special organ used to store energy. The energy may have been used to help dinosaurs move their back legs and tails.

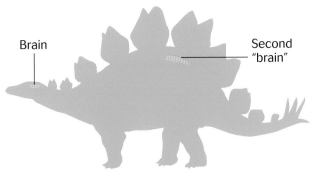

Brain

Second "brain"

In this diagram, the shaded area near the Stegosaurus' tail was probably an energy store.

Clever dinosaurs

Carnivorous dinosaurs had the biggest brains for their body size and were the most intelligent dinosaurs. They needed such big brains, together with keen senses, to track their prey. Small carnivore Troodon was probably the most intelligent dinosaur of all.

This meat-eating Deinonychus is intelligent compared to most dinosaurs.

Dinosaur senses

Dinosaurs needed keen senses to hunt prey and to spot predators so that they could run away before they were attacked.

Troodons, such as this one, have excellent eyesight, which makes it easier for them to find prey.

Seeing double

Most dinosaurs had eyes on either side of their heads. This gave them two different views of the world. They could see almost all the way around them, but weren't able to judge distances as well as we can.

The shaded areas show how much most dinosaurs could see without moving their heads.

The big picture

Troodon had both eyes on the front of its head. Each eye gave it a slightly different view of the world from the other. But normally, with both eyes open, those views would be combined into a single image. This sort of vision is called stereoscopic vision. Animals with stereoscopic vision are generally good at seeing depth and judging distances.

Troodons couldn't see behind them without turning their heads.

Detecting objects

When people look at grass they can usually see that it is green. Birds and reptiles see things as humans do, but many other animals can only see in black and white. We don't know how dinosaurs saw the world. But if they saw things as birds do, they would have been much better at detecting objects than animals that only see in black and white.

Ⓕ Internet links

For links to websites where you can explore a gallery of dinosaurs and play a game that shows you how your vision changes when you look through one eye at a time, go to **www.usborne-quicklinks.com**

Sense of smell

Tyrannosaurus rex had a very keen sense of smell. Using special equipment, scientists have been able to look inside a Tyrannosaurus rex's fossilized head. They discovered that the part of its brain devoted to its sense of smell was very big. Having a good sense of smell would have made it easier for it to find prey.

Hearing sounds

Dinosaurs had holes behind their eyes which were their ears. By studying the fossilized cases that surrounded their brains, paleontologists calculate that dinosaurs had a fairly good sense of hearing, but probably relied more on their other senses.

Tyrannosaurus rex's brain was about 0.3m (1ft) across. The part devoted to smell was the size of a grapefruit.

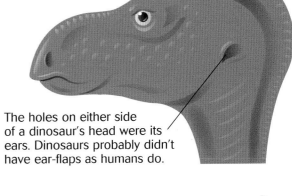

The holes on either side of a dinosaur's head were its ears. Dinosaurs probably didn't have ear-flaps as humans do.

Living in groups

Some plant-eating dinosaurs lived together in large groups, called herds. By living together, dinosaurs could protect each other.

Any plants that are in the way of this sauropod herd are likely either to be eaten or trampled.

On the move

Herds of dinosaurs may have covered huge distances, looking for food. Each year, they would have made journeys to places where the weather was warmer. This is called migration. Many modern animals, such as buffaloes and some birds, make journeys like this.

ⓕ **Internet links**

For links to websites where you can watch herds of Triceratops and hadrasaurs, and read about fossil evidence of dinosaurs living in herds, go to **www.usborne-quicklinks.com**

Making a mess

Groups of large dinosaurs stirred up the earth as they moved. This is called dinoturbation. They also trampled many trees and plants that were in their way. Surprisingly, this may have helped some plants to spread. Flowering plants tend to grow back more quickly after being squashed into the earth than non-flowering plants do. They could spread quickly, covering ground where non-flowering plants once grew.

Flowering magnolias, like this one, first appeared toward the end of the Mesozoic era.

 Fact: Tracks left by groups of sauropods show that the largest animals were at the front of the herd.

Attracting attention

Dinosaurs that lived in groups probably had some way of communicating with each other. Some dinosaurs would have made noises to attract each other's attention. For example, Diplodocus might have communicated using its whip-like tail. By flicking it very quickly, it could have made a loud booming noise.

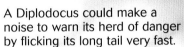

★
A Diplodocus could make a noise to warn its herd of danger by flicking its long tail very fast.

Hunting in packs

For some time, fossil evidence has suggested that some smaller meat-eating dinosaurs, such as Deinonychus, lived and hunted in packs. But, recently, scientists have discovered the skeletons of huge adult Tyrannosaurus rex along with their young. Perhaps they too lived and hunted together.

A family group of Deinonychus dinosaurs

Extraordinary eggs

S cientists think all baby dinosaurs grew in eggs laid by their mothers, as birds do. As many as 30 eggs have been found in a single nest, but they may have been laid by more than one mother.

A hadrosaur's egg

Keeping warm

Eggs need to be incubated (kept at the right temperature). Birds do this by sitting on them. But most dinosaurs probably buried their eggs to incubate them, perhaps because they were too big to sit on the eggs without crushing them.

A dinosaur would have carefully covered its eggs with plants and sand, to make a mound.

The plants on the mound gave out heat as they rotted down, helping to incubate the eggs. ★

Building nests

Most dinosaurs made nests to keep their eggs safe. They did this by scraping out a hole in the ground, or by building a muddy rim on the ground to keep the eggs in place. Dinosaur eggs have been found laid out in neat circles, and in straight lines.

Here you can see how the muddy rim of this Troodon nest stops the eggs from rolling away.

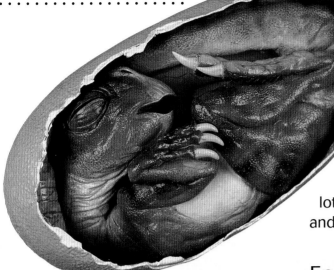

Whose baby?

Amazingly, scientists have found fossilized eggs with fossilized baby dinosaurs still inside them. These help paleontologists to identify which eggs belonged to which dinosaur, and tell us a lot about how baby dinosaurs grew and developed.

This little baby dinosaur isn't ready to break out of its egg yet. It stays inside, feeding off the yolk in the egg.

 Internet links

For a link to a website where you can hunt for dinosaur eggs around the world and examine a dinosaur egg online, go to **www.usborne-quicklinks.com**

Enormous eggs

The biggest dinosaur egg found so far is about 45cm (18in) long. That may sound big, but its parents could have been a hundred times as big as this. Scientists think that if dinosaur eggs had been any bigger than 50cm (20in), their shells would have been too thick for babies to break out of them.

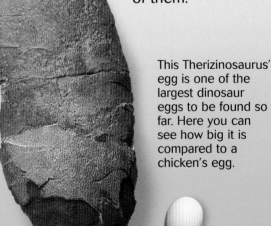

This Therizinosaurus' egg is one of the largest dinosaur eggs to be found so far. Here you can see how big it is compared to a chicken's egg.

Safe inside

Dinosaur eggs contained yolk, which gave the babies inside all the food they needed. The shells of the eggs had tiny holes, or pores, in them. These let fresh air in and bad gases out of the eggs, allowing the baby dinosaurs to breathe freely.

A Therizinosaurus' egg   A chicken's egg

Fact: Dinosaur eggs had a chemical in them called calcium which helped the babies' bones to grow and become strong.

Dinosaur babies

When baby dinosaurs had grown enough to be able to survive outside their eggs, they had to break out. This is called hatching.

Hatching out

This shows how a baby dinosaur would have begun to hatch out of its egg.

After chipping all the way around the egg, the baby would finally be able to hatch.

★

Baby dinosaurs had a special tooth which they used to help them break out of their eggs. First they chipped at their eggs with the tooth to make a small hole. Then they chipped all around the egg, until it split open and they could push themselves all the way out.

All alone

Some baby dinosaurs were independent when they hatched, and were fully able to take care of themselves. They left the nest very soon after hatching to look for food and to hide from predators. They knew what food to look for and where to look for it, without being taught by their parents.

Growing up

Scientists don't know for certain how fast dinosaurs grew, but they can make guesses based on how fast modern reptiles grow. Large dinosaurs probably took 10–20 years to become adults.

A nest of newly-hatched Orodromeus dinosaurs begin to explore their world.

Good mothers

Not all baby dinosaurs were independent as soon as they had hatched. Some scientists think that newly-hatched Maiasaura babies were only 30cm (1ft) long. They would have been too weak to take care of themselves for the first few weeks of their lives. Their mothers protected them and brought them food until they were big and strong enough to leave their nests.

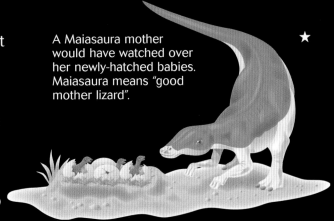

A Maiasaura mother would have watched over her newly-hatched babies. Maiasaura means "good mother lizard".

ⓕ Internet links

For links to websites where you can watch video clips about baby dinosaurs and see a picture of a real fossilized dinosaur baby, go to **www.usborne-quicklinks.com**

Sturdy stegosaurs .....

Stegosaurs were large herbivorous dinosaurs, famous for having very small brains. Even so, they were a very successful group of dinosaurs, surviving for over 60 million years.

Heads to the ground

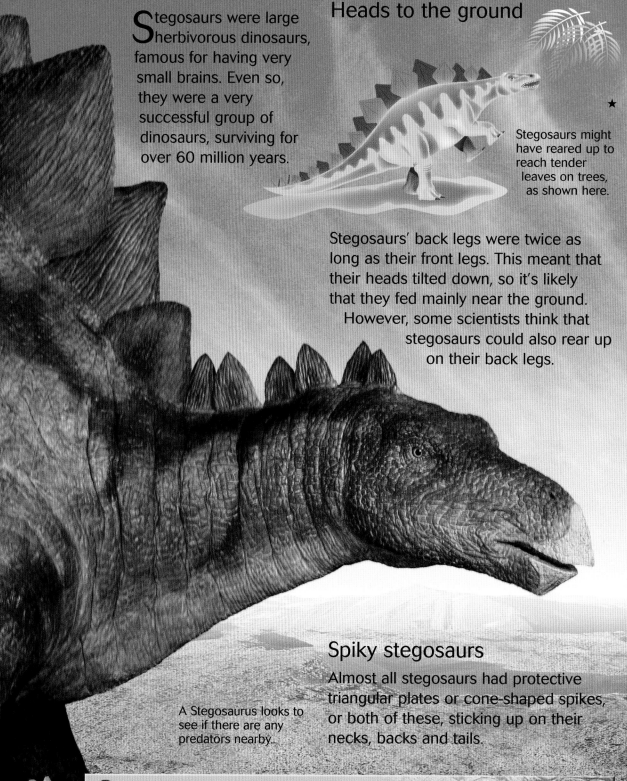

Stegosaurs might have reared up to reach tender leaves on trees, as shown here.

Stegosaurs' back legs were twice as long as their front legs. This meant that their heads tilted down, so it's likely that they fed mainly near the ground. However, some scientists think that stegosaurs could also rear up on their back legs.

A Stegosaurus looks to see if there are any predators nearby.

Spiky stegosaurs

Almost all stegosaurs had protective triangular plates or cone-shaped spikes, or both of these, sticking up on their necks, backs and tails.

Fact: No two plates from a single stegosaur were exactly the same shape or size.

Strong but slow

Stegosaurs had strong leg bones to carry their great weight, but had weak leg muscles. This meant they couldn't run very fast. Instead of running away from predators, they could defend themselves with their tail spikes.

Hot plates

The plates on stegosaurs' backs had tiny tubes in them with blood inside. Scientists disagree about what the plates were for.

This is what a stegosaur's plate looked like inside.

Some scientists think that in hot sunshine stegosaurs' plates could have soaked up the heat, making the stegosaur warmer.

Turning pink

A few scientists think that stegosaurs may have been able to pump blood into their plates to make them turn pink. They might have done this when they wanted to attract a mate or frighten an enemy.

This shows how an angry Stegosaurus might have swung its spiky tail to scare off an Allosaurus.

Here you can see how this Stegosaurus' head tilts down toward the ground.

★

Mighty sauropods ....

Some of the biggest animals ever to have lived belonged to a group of dinosaurs called sauropods. They were all small-brained plant-eaters, and walked on four legs.

Amazingly long

Sauropods ranged in size from the 5m (17ft) long Magyarosaurus to the incredible 40m (130ft) Amphicoelias fragillimus. It's possible that there are bigger sauropods still waiting to be discovered. No one knows why some sauropods grew to be so big when others didn't.

These sauropods are so big that they overheat easily in hot sunshine. They are looking for water to cool them down.

Swimming sauropods?

Sauropods' nostrils were on top of their heads. Scientists once thought that they lived underwater in lakes, keeping their nostrils above the water so that they could breathe. In fact, sauropods couldn't have lived like this. Below the surface, the weight of the water would have damaged their lungs, causing the sauropods to die. Scientists now believe that sauropods lived on dry land.

Internet links

For links to websites with sauropod video clips and all kinds of fascinating facts and figures, go to **www.usborne-quicklinks.com**

Long necks

Sauropods had extremely long necks and small heads. Their long necks would have enabled them to reach out for plants over a large area, without moving the rest of their bodies. This meant that they could save a lot of energy while feeding.

Sauroposeidon had the longest neck of all sauropods. Its neck was about 15m (50ft) long. That's about eight times as long as a giraffe's neck.

★

Giraffes have the longest necks of all living animals, but their necks are short when compared with the necks of sauropods.

Big-hearted sauropods

Brains need a good supply of oxygen to work properly. A brain gets this from blood, which is pumped around the body by the heart. Sauropods would have had big, strong hearts, so that enough blood could be pumped all the way up their extremely long necks to their heads, and down to the tips of their tails.

Honking hadrosaurs ....

Hadrosaurs are sometimes known as duck-billed dinosaurs because they had flat, hard beaks, a little like ducks' beaks. They were plant-eating dinosaurs and have been described by one scientist as "cattle of the Cretaceous period", as they lived in herds and were very common at that time.

Hollow honking tubes

Many hadrosaurs had horn-like ridges, or crests, on their heads. Some hadrosaurs, such as Parasaurolophus, had crests that were hollow and attached to tubes inside their noses. Scientists think that they may have been able to make loud bellowing noises by blowing air down them.

This herd of Parasaurolophus is on the move. They usually walk on their two back legs, but sometimes walk on all fours while looking for food.

Internet links

For links to websites where you can hear how a Parasaurolophus may have sounded and meet other creatures of the Cretaceous period, go to **www.usborne-quicklinks.com**

All sorts of crests

Hadrosaurs' crests varied in shape and size, according to the type of hadrosaur, whether it was male or female, or young or old. The different shapes and sizes may have enabled hadrosaurs to recognize other members of the same species.

Here you can see how different hadrosaurs' crests looked.

Corythosaurus   Saurolophus   Tsintaosaurus   ★

Beaks and chewing

Hadrosaurs ate berries, flowering plants and evergreen plants. They could slice off the toughest leaves with their sharp beaks.

Their jaws were perfect for chewing. They could move them back and forward and from side to side, as well as up and down. They had up to 200 teeth in their mouths. People only have 32 at most.

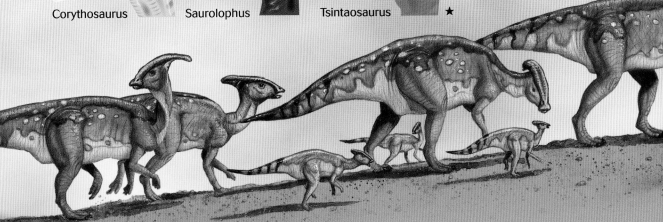

Running away together

Hadrosaurs could run quickly on their strong, back legs. At the first sign of danger, a hadrosaur could bellow to warn the rest of the herd and the whole herd could escape by running away. This was very important as they had no special means of defending themselves against an attacker.

Out in the cold

Hadrosaurs lived in many different parts of the world. Some lived in an area known as the Arctic Circle, where it is very cold, and completely dark during the winter months. When hadrosaurs lived, these regions were not as cold as they are now, but they would still have had to survive in cool weather, as well as in total darkness for some of the year.

Terrible tyrannosaurs

Tyrannosaurs were large, ferocious meat-eating dinosaurs that walked on two legs. They included one of the biggest carnivorous land animals – Tyrannosaurus rex.

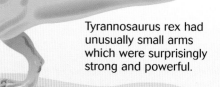

Tyrannosaurus rex had unusually small arms which were surprisingly strong and powerful.

Fast runners?

Tyrannosaurs ranged from 9–15m (30–50ft) long and weighed from 3–6 tonnes (3–6 tons). Because they were so heavy, you might think that they wouldn't have been able to run very fast. But tyrannosaurs had long, powerful legs which probably enabled them to run fairly quickly for creatures of their size.

Little arms

Although tyrannosaurs had long back legs, their arms were very short. In fact, their arms were so short that they couldn't even reach their mouths with them, and so couldn't have used them to help with eating. Scientists still aren't sure what tyrannosaurs used their arms for.

This tyrannosaur is hunting for food. It preys on plant-eating dinosaurs that come to the forest to look for food themselves.

Falling down

Paleontologists have found the skeleton of an Albertosaurus, a tyrannosaur, with bones that had broken, and then healed again. They think that the injuries may have happened when the dinosaur tripped and fell over while running very fast. Because it had such small arms, the Albertosaurus wouldn't have been able to break its fall by stretching them out.

Big biters

Tyrannosaurus rex had 18cm (11in) long teeth and a ferocious bite. Paleontologists can tell how strong Tyrannosaurus rex's bite was by examining bite-marks it left in the bones of other dinosaurs. They estimate that its bite was more powerful than that of any living land animal.

This Tyrannosaurus rex has about 50 razor-sharp teeth.

Internet links

For links to websites where you can explore a clickable picture of Tyrannosaurus rex and decide if it was a scavenger or a predator then try lots of other fun tyrannosaur activities, go to **www.usborne-quicklinks.com**

Fighting each other

Tyrannosaurs didn't just bite other animals. Scientists have found Tyrannosaurus rex bones with bite marks in them that were made by other tyrannosaurs.

One tyrannosaur died when its neck bone was bitten all the way through by another tyrannosaur. Large chunks of bone had been ripped out of it. Some scientists think that the dead tyrannosaur may have been partially eaten by the tyrannosaur that attacked it.

Tyrannosaurs would have fought each other as they competed to live and hunt in the same area.

Dreadful dromaeosaurs ....

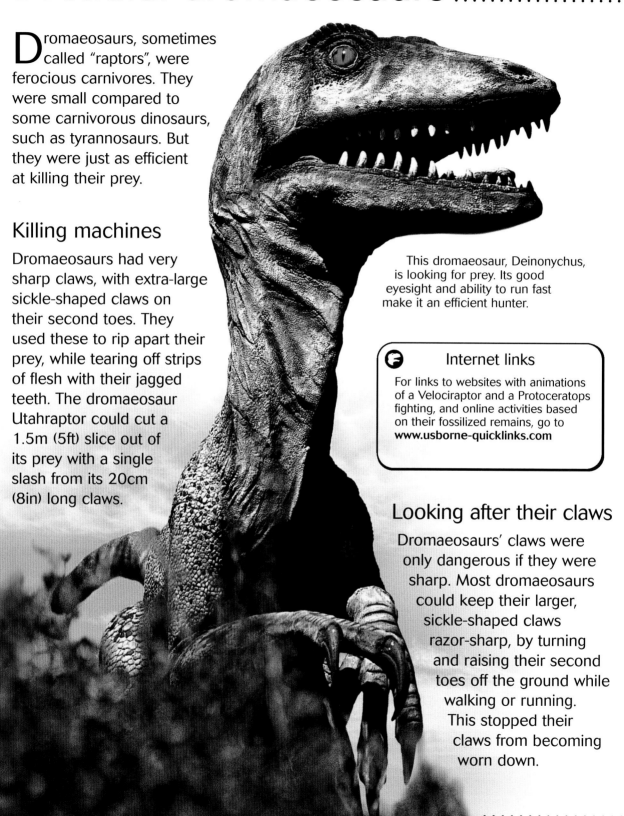

Dromaeosaurs, sometimes called "raptors", were ferocious carnivores. They were small compared to some carnivorous dinosaurs, such as tyrannosaurs. But they were just as efficient at killing their prey.

Killing machines

Dromaeosaurs had very sharp claws, with extra-large sickle-shaped claws on their second toes. They used these to rip apart their prey, while tearing off strips of flesh with their jagged teeth. The dromaeosaur Utahraptor could cut a 1.5m (5ft) slice out of its prey with a single slash from its 20cm (8in) long claws.

This dromaeosaur, Deinonychus, is looking for prey. Its good eyesight and ability to run fast make it an efficient hunter.

Internet links

For links to websites with animations of a Velociraptor and a Protoceratops fighting, and online activities based on their fossilized remains, go to **www.usborne-quicklinks.com**

Looking after their claws

Dromaeosaurs' claws were only dangerous if they were sharp. Most dromaeosaurs could keep their larger, sickle-shaped claws razor-sharp, by turning and raising their second toes off the ground while walking or running. This stopped their claws from becoming worn down.

Balancing act

Dromaeosaurs had long, stiff tails, which they used to help them turn quickly while running. They also used them to help them balance while they stood on one leg. Standing on one leg, they could use their other leg to kick and slash at their prey.

Deinonychus could probably run and jump up at its prey to knock it to the ground. This shows how it leapt up to attack.

★

Fight to the death

Scientists have found the fossilized skeletons of a Velociraptor, a type of dromaeosaur, and a herbivorous Protoceratops locked together in combat. Before one could defeat the other, they were both killed, perhaps by a sudden sandstorm that buried them both and killed them almost instantly.

Before birds

Scientists find dromaeosaurs very interesting because they had many features in common with birds. Some dromaeosaurs may even have had feathers. Many scientists think that dromaeosaurs were the direct ancestors of birds.

A Velociraptor and a Protoceratops in battle, moments before they are buried in a sandstorm

Terrors of the seas ....

While dinosaurs lived on the land, other amazing prehistoric animals lived in the seas. Like the dinosaurs, many of these creatures were reptiles. They were related to dinosaurs, but only very distantly. All of these creatures died out, along with the dinosaurs, 65 million years ago.

Born to swim

Ichthyosaurs swam through the water, moving their tails from side to side like fish. They didn't lay eggs as many other reptiles did, but instead gave birth to babies in the sea.

Ichthyosaurs were strong, fast swimmers.

Leaving the land

About 290 million years ago, some land reptiles began to spend more and more time in the sea. Gradually, new species developed, with bodies that were adapted to these new surroundings. But they never learned to breathe under water. Instead, they came up to the surface for air every now and then.

Hunters of the deep

Ichthyosaurs had very large eyes which helped them to see well in the dark. They may have dived down to the murky depths of the oceans, where there was little light to see by, looking for food, such as squid, ammonites and fish.

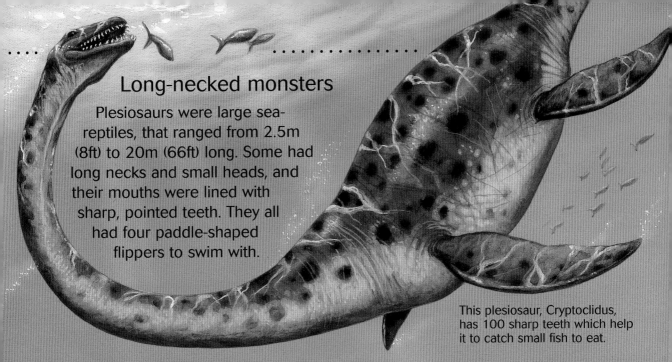

Long-necked monsters

Plesiosaurs were large sea-reptiles, that ranged from 2.5m (8ft) to 20m (66ft) long. Some had long necks and small heads, and their mouths were lined with sharp, pointed teeth. They all had four paddle-shaped flippers to swim with.

This plesiosaur, Cryptoclidus, has 100 sharp teeth which help it to catch small fish to eat.

(F) Internet links

For a link to a website where you can watch video clips and read fact files on lots of prehistoric sea creatures, including a Liopleurodon, go to **www.usborne-quicklinks.com**

Jurassic jaws

Pliosaurs were a type of plesiosaur. They had shorter necks than other plesiosaurs, and huge heads and deadly teeth. Pliosaurs were fearsome predators. They could hunt by tracking their prey's scent.

If a sea creature had recently been nearby, its scent would still be in the water. Pliosaurs could detect the scent by filtering water through their mouths and out of their nostrils.

This is a Liopleurodon, which is a type of pliosaur. Here, it's chasing a baby Ichthyosaur, but it can easily catch and eat an adult with its long, sharp teeth.

Fact: Ichthyosaur babies were born tail-first. If they had been born head-first, they would have drowned before they could reach the surface to take their first breath.

Masters of the skies

P̲terosaurs were winged reptiles that
lived at the same time as dinosaurs.
They were only very distantly related to
dinosaurs and despite their appearance
were even more distantly related to birds.

Wings for flying

Pterosaurs usually flew by flapping their
wings. This is called powered flight.
Larger pterosaurs with bigger wings may
have flapped just to get up into the air.
Once in the air, they could glide,
rather than flap, to save energy.

Large, but light

Although some pterosaurs were as small
as ducks, many were so big it seems
amazing that they could fly at all. In fact,
they were surprisingly light for their size.
They had very small bodies compared
to their wing-size and had thin,
hollow bones.

Pterosaurs, such as this
Pteranodon, have wings
made of tough, leathery skin.

Giants in the air

Quetzalcoatlus was one of the biggest
pterosaurs. With a huge wingspan of
10m (33ft), it was the size of a small
plane. Recently, scientists have found
the fossil of an even bigger pterosaur in
Spain. It had a wingspan of 11m (36ft).

This shows how big Quetzalcoatlus
was compared to a small, one-engine plane.

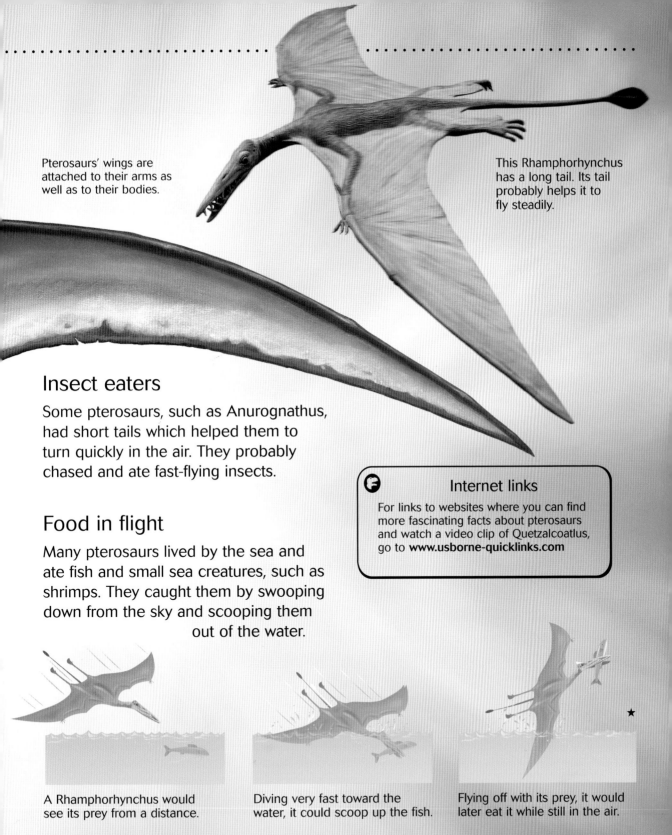

Pterosaurs' wings are attached to their arms as well as to their bodies.

This Rhamphorhynchus has a long tail. Its tail probably helps it to fly steadily.

Insect eaters

Some pterosaurs, such as Anurognathus, had short tails which helped them to turn quickly in the air. They probably chased and ate fast-flying insects.

Food in flight

Many pterosaurs lived by the sea and ate fish and small sea creatures, such as shrimps. They caught them by swooping down from the sky and scooping them out of the water.

Ⓕ Internet links

For links to websites where you can find more fascinating facts about pterosaurs and watch a video clip of Quetzalcoatlus, go to **www.usborne-quicklinks.com**

A Rhamphorhynchus would see its prey from a distance.

Diving very fast toward the water, it could scoop up the fish.

Flying off with its prey, it would later eat it while still in the air.

 Fact: Some pterosaurs had fur on their bodies to keep them warm.

Death of the dinosaurs

About 65 million years ago, all the dinosaurs and many other animals became extinct, or died out. Nobody knows for sure why this happened, but scientists have two main theories to try to explain it.

Erupting volcanoes

At the end of the Mesozoic era, volcanoes were erupting all over the world. When a volcano erupts, it spurts out very hot, liquid rock called lava. The lava flows away from the volcano, destroying everything in its path. This would have killed many animals and plants, but on its own it was not enough to kill all of them.

This slow-flowing lava continues to cause damage long after the volcano first erupts.

Poisonous clouds

Erupting volcanoes send dust and poisonous chemicals into the air. The chemicals may have killed baby dinosaurs growing in their eggs. If there was enough dust, it might have blocked out sunlight, making the Earth cooler. Animals needing warm weather would have died.

Disaster chain

The poisonous chemicals and the lack of sunlight would have caused many plants to die. About two-thirds of all known dinosaurs were plant-eaters. Without plants, they would have starved to death. If the plant-eaters died, soon there would have been no animals left for the meat-eaters to eat, and so they too would have died.

Meteorite menace

Around the time that the dinosaurs died out, a giant lump of rock, 10km (5 miles) wide, hurtled through space and collided with the Earth. A lump of rock or metal that falls from space is called a meteorite. Near Mexico, a huge crater, or hole in the ground, has been found under the sea. This is where the meteorite hit the Earth.

Internet links

For links to websites where you can watch an animation of an asteroid impact, explore other dinosaur extinction theories and see which creatures survived, go to **www.usborne-quicklinks.com**

This shows how a meteorite may have looked as it crashed into the Earth.

Impact!

Upon hitting the Earth, the meteorite would have exploded, creating a dust cloud and causing earthquakes, fires and hurricanes. The impact would have made volcanoes erupt. Clouds of dust would have blocked out the sunlight. Plants and then dinosaurs would have died.

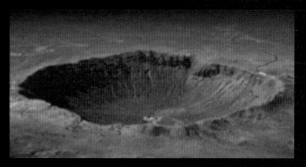

This is a crater called the Barringer crater in the U.S.A. It's 1.2km (0.7 miles) wide. Amazingly, the crater made by the meteorite that may have killed the dinosaurs was probably 150 times as wide.

Mysterious survivors

Puzzlingly, not all life on Earth was wiped out along with the dinosaurs. All animals measuring over 3m (10ft) long died, but some smaller animals, such as all insects and some birds, lizards and sea creatures, survived. Why some animals became extinct while others didn't is still a mystery.

Fact: People have only been on the Earth for 2.5 million years, but dinosaurs were around for 165 million years. That's 66 times as long as people have lived.

49

Design a dinosaur ....

In the movie Jurassic Park, dinosaurs are brought to life again, but what about in real life? Some scientists think that they really will be able to recreate dinosaurs. To try to do this, they need some dinosaur DNA.

Design for life

DNA is a very complicated chemical which is found in every living thing. It's like a plan, or design, because it contains all the information about what an animal or plant needs to live. If scientists have enough of an animal or plant's DNA, they can use it to make an exact copy. The copy is called a clone and it has exactly the same DNA as the original.

The prehistoric insects preserved in this amber could contain dinosaur DNA.

Recreating a dinosaur

Scientists have found pieces of amber (fossilized tree resin) with insects preserved inside them. If one of these insects had fed on dinosaur blood, and some of that blood had been preserved, scientists might be able to find some dinosaur DNA. They could then use it to try to make dinosaur clones. This is what happened in Jurassic Park.

Will it work?

So far, although scientists have cloned living animals, no one has managed to clone a dinosaur. DNA doesn't last forever and many scientists think that dinosaurs died too long ago for enough of their DNA to have survived. But this doesn't mean that other, more recent, prehistoric animals, such as mammoths, can't be cloned.

This is a model of a section of DNA. Actual DNA is so tiny that you need a very powerful electron microscope to see it.

Dinosaurs alive?

It is very unlikely that scientists will ever clone dinosaurs, but could there be dinosaurs still living today? In 1938, a type of prehistoric fish called a coelacanth was found alive. Previously, scientists thought that it had become extinct at the end of the Mesozoic era. From time to time, people claim to have seen animals that look like dinosaurs, pterosaurs and plesiosaurs. But there is no good evidence that such animals really exist.

Ⓕ Internet links

For links to websites where you can click on pieces of amber to see what's inside them, explore a fun guide to cloning and learn more about the coelacanth, a prehistoric fish, go to **www.usborne-quicklinks.com**

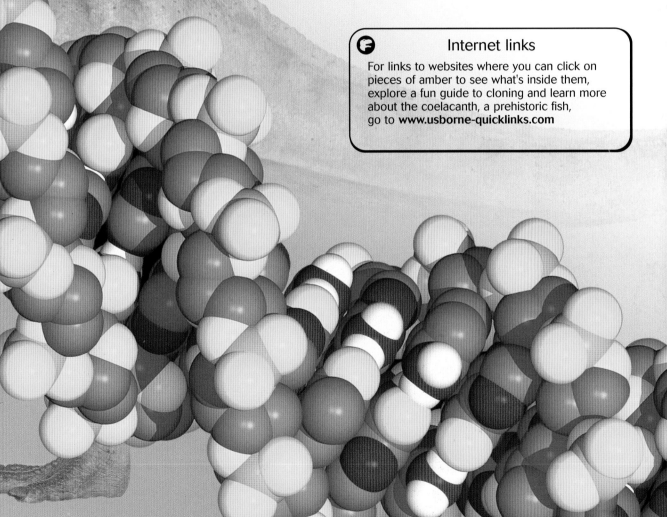

Today's dinosaurs

Most paleontologists believe that birds are descended from dinosaurs. This is because birds and dinosaurs have many features in common. In fact, they are so similar that many scientists regard birds as a type of dinosaur.

Early bird

One of the earliest known birds is Archaeopteryx. It had feathers like a modern bird, but its tail was long and it had sharp teeth like a reptile. It could probably fly, but not very far and not very well.

An Archaeopteryx perches in a tree, ready to swoop down on small animals for food.

Learning to fly

Scientists aren't sure how the first birds learned to fly. Some think that they spent much of their time in trees. Perhaps they developed simple wings to help them glide from tree to tree, or to slow them down if they fell. Eventually, they somehow developed the ability to flap their wings.

Taking off

Some scientists think that birds first flew while running very fast along the ground. As they ran, they might have flapped their wings to help them to run faster. While leaping into the air to catch insects for food, perhaps they learned to fly.

An early bird might have run fast, flapping its wings.

Seeing an insect it might have leapt up to catch it.

A breeze would help to lift the bird a little way off the ground.

Bird-like dinosaurs

Recent discoveries show that Archaeopteryx was very similar to some small meat-eating dinosaurs. Caudipteryx and Sinosauropteryx even had feathers. This and other similarities suggest that these dinosaurs might have been the direct ancestors of birds.

Caudipteryx is a fast-running feathered carnivore.

Ⓕ Internet links

For links to websites where you can build an Archaeopteryx online and discover how birds evolved from dinosaurs, go to **www.usborne-quicklinks.com**

 Fact: Feathers would have helped bird-like dinosaurs to keep warm.

Latest discoveries ....

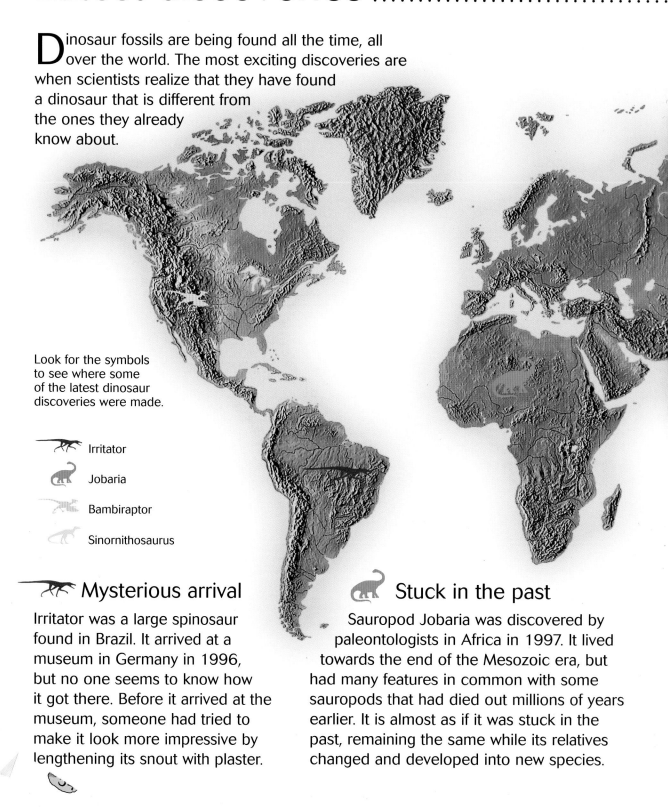

Dinosaur fossils are being found all the time, all over the world. The most exciting discoveries are when scientists realize that they have found a dinosaur that is different from the ones they already know about.

Look for the symbols to see where some of the latest dinosaur discoveries were made.

Irritator

Jobaria

Bambiraptor

Sinornithosaurus

Mysterious arrival

Irritator was a large spinosaur found in Brazil. It arrived at a museum in Germany in 1996, but no one seems to know how it got there. Before it arrived at the museum, someone had tried to make it look more impressive by lengthening its snout with plaster.

Stuck in the past

Sauropod Jobaria was discovered by paleontologists in Africa in 1997. It lived towards the end of the Mesozoic era, but had many features in common with some sauropods that had died out millions of years earlier. It is almost as if it was stuck in the past, remaining the same while its relatives changed and developed into new species.

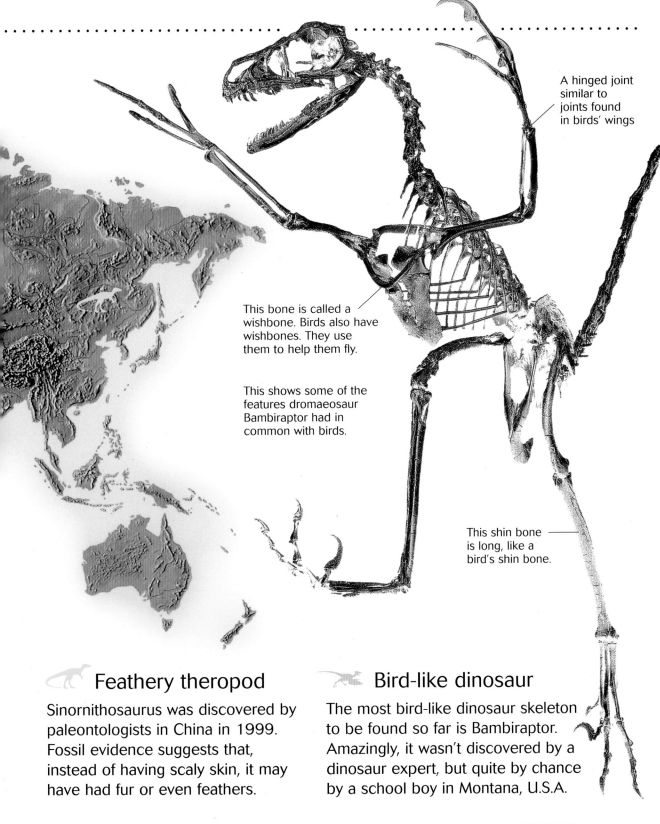

A hinged joint similar to joints found in birds' wings

This bone is called a wishbone. Birds also have wishbones. They use them to help them fly.

This shows some of the features dromaeosaur Bambiraptor had in common with birds.

This shin bone is long, like a bird's shin bone.

Feathery theropod

Sinornithosaurus was discovered by paleontologists in China in 1999. Fossil evidence suggests that, instead of having scaly skin, it may have had fur or even feathers.

Bird-like dinosaur

The most bird-like dinosaur skeleton to be found so far is Bambiraptor. Amazingly, it wasn't discovered by a dinosaur expert, but quite by chance by a school boy in Montana, U.S.A.

Fact: Amazingly, nearly all the dinosaurs discovered so far have been found in the last 25 years.

Dinosaur families

T his chart shows how some of the different kinds of dinosaurs were related to each other. For example, if you look at the top right hand side of the tree, you can see that Caudipteryx, Ingenia and Oviraptor all belonged to the same family of oviraptorosaurs. These are part of the larger group, Maniraptorans, which in turn belong to an even larger group called theropods.

Corythosaurus

Parasaurolophus

Corythosaurus

Maiasaura

Triceratops

Styracosaurus

Protoceratops

Protoceratops

HADROSAURS

Iguanodon

Pachycephalosaurus

Hypsilophodon

ANKYLOSAURS

STEGOSAURS

CERATOPSIANS

ORNITHOPODS

Scelidosaurus

THYREOPHORANS

Scelidosaurus

ORNITHISCHIANS

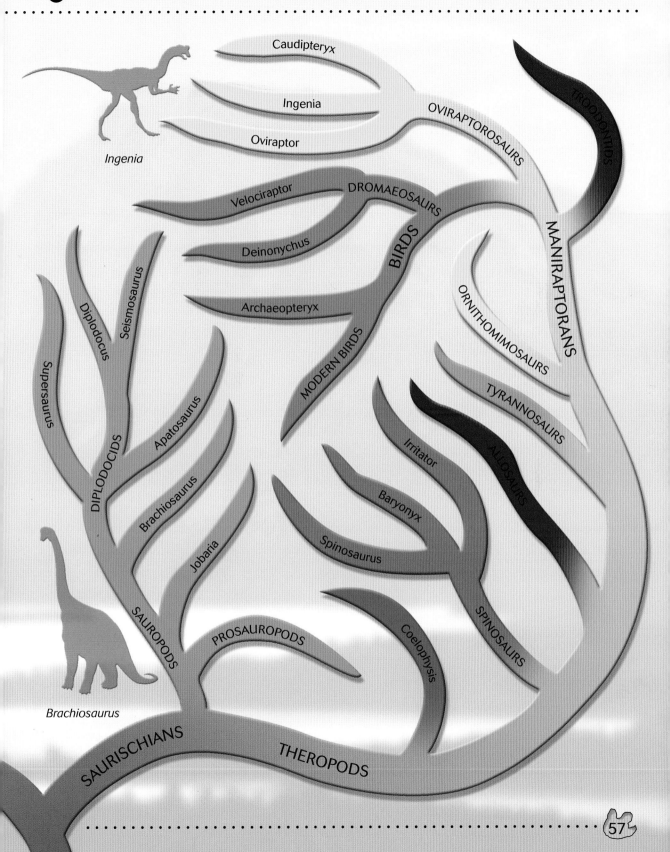

Caudipteryx

Ingenia

Oviraptor

Ingenia

OVIRAPTOROSAURS

TROODONTIDS

Velociraptor

DROMAEOSAURS

Deinonychus

BIRDS

Archaeopteryx

MANIRAPTORANS

Diplodocus

Seismosaurus

MODERN BIRDS

ORNITHOMIMOSAURS

Supersaurus

Apatosaurus

TYRANNOSAURS

Irritator

ALLOSAURS

DIPLODOCIDS

Brachiosaurus

Baryonyx

Jobaria

Spinosaurus

Brachiosaurus

SAUROPODS

PROSAUROPODS

Coelophysis

SPINOSAURS

SAURISCHIANS

THEROPODS

57

Dinosaur data

There are many things about dinosaurs that we may never discover. Fossils give us valuable clues, but they can't tell us everything we want to know. But with the help of some of the amazing discoveries that have been made, paleontologists can still form theories about what dinosaurs were really like.

 Although many scientists think that birds are descended from dromaeosaur dinosaurs, some scientists disagree. Instead, they say that dromaeosaurs are, in fact, descended from early birds. They believe that dromaeosaurs were actually flightless birds.

 Scientists aren't sure what Triceratops' bony frills were for. Some think they may have used them to protect themselves. Others suggest that the frills may have helped Triceratops to keep cool.

A Triceratops

 In North America, paleontologists have discovered fossilized footprints of a dinosaur with webbed feet. But they don't belong to any dinosaur they know about.

 Ceratopsian dinosaur Torosaurus had the biggest skull of any land animal that has ever lived. Its skull was nearly 3m (8ft) long, which was half the length of its entire body.

 Dinosaurs with long tails, such as Diplodocus, may have used their tails to help them swim across water.

 Scientists calculate that if an animal were heavier than about 203 tonnes (200 tons), it would be too heavy to move. The biggest dinosaurs probably weighed just a little less than this.

Bony neck frill

Some fossilized dinosaur dung has tiny holes in it. These were created by insects, such as beetles, which ate the dung.

 People have been discovering dinosaur fossils for many centuries, but it wasn't until the 19th century that they realized just what they were. The first dinosaur to be recognized as a dinosaur was named Megalosaurus in 1824.

 The skeletons of some meat-eating Coelophysis had the fossilized bones of baby Coelophysis in the area where their stomachs were. Scientists think that the adults may have eaten the babies.

 Gallimimus was probably the fastest dinosaur. Scientists estimate that it could run at a speed of 56kph (35mph).

 Very large plant-eating dinosaurs tended to overheat and probably spent much of their time trying to cool down, for example, by bathing in water.

 With 220 teeth, theropod Pelecanimimus had more teeth than any other theropod. This is remarkable because Pelecanimimus belonged to a group of dinosaurs famous for not having any teeth at all.

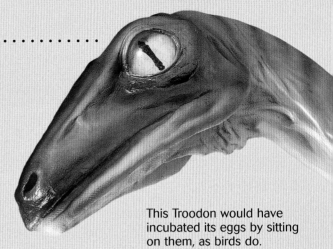

This Troodon would have incubated its eggs by sitting on them, as birds do.

 Not all dinosaurs buried their eggs to incubate them. Some dinosaurs, such as Troodon, sat on their eggs, as modern birds do, keeping the eggs at the right temperature with their bodies.

 Therizinosaurus had the longest claws of any dinosaur. They were more than 70cm (27in) long.

 Scientists can guess whether or not herbivorous dinosaurs ate plants near the ground by looking at their teeth. Plants near the ground have grit and dust on them which leave scratch marks on teeth.

Internet links

For links to websites where you can find out lots more about dinosaurs, go to
www.usborne-quicklinks.com

Website 1   The latest news about dinosaurs.
Website 2   Test-yourself dinosaur quiz.
Website 3   Play a game about dinosaur imposters.
Website 4   Dinosaur things to make and do.

Glossary

This glossary explains some of the words you might come across when reading about dinosaurs. Words in *italic type* have their own entries elsewhere in the glossary.

amber Fossilized tree resin which sometimes contains preserved small animal and plant remains.

avian dinosaur Another name for a bird. Birds are believed to be the descendants of dinosaurs which means that they are, in fact, a type of dinosaur.

body fossil A *fossil* of any part of an animal or plant, such as a bone or a leaf.

carnivore An animal that only eats meat.

clone To make an exact copy of an animal using its *DNA*.

crest A horn-like ridge on the top of an animal's head. Some hadrosaurs had crests.

Cretaceous period Period of time 144–65 million years ago.

dinoturbation The stirring up of soil caused by herds of very large dinosaurs as they moved across the land.

DNA Deoxyribonucleic acid. This is a very complex chemical that's in every living thing. Each piece of DNA contains a huge amount of information about the living thing it belongs to.

extinction The death of all of the members of a *species* of animal. This usually happens gradually.

fossil The remains or trace of a plant or an animal preserved in rock.

fossilize To turn into a *fossil*.

gastrolith A stomach stone. Dinosaurs swallowed very hard stones, such as quartzite, to help them break down food.

genus (plural: genera) A group of animal or plant *species* that are very closely related to each other.

gizzard A part of a dinosaur's guts where food is broken down.

gout A painful disease of the joints which some dinosaurs suffered from.

hatch To break out of an egg.

herbivore An animal that only eats plants.

herd A group of animals that live and feed together.

incubate To keep eggs at the right temperature so that the babies inside can grow and develop.

Jurassic period Period of time 208–144 million years ago.

lava Very hot, liquid rock that comes out of volcanoes when they erupt.

mass extinction The death of lots of *species* of animals or plants at the same time.

Mesozoic era A period of time 240–65 million years ago, when dinosaurs lived. It is divided into the *Triassic, Jurassic* and *Cretaceous periods*.

meteorite A rock from space that falls to Earth.

migrate To move from one place to another at certain times of the year, to look for warmer temperatures, or to find food.

omnivore An animal that eats both plants and meat.

ornithischian One of the two main groups of dinosaurs. Ornithischian dinosaurs had hips shaped like birds' hips.

pack A group of meat-eating animals that live and hunt together.

paleontologist Someone who studies fossils.

paleontology The study of fossils.

plesiosaurs A group of *reptiles* that lived in the seas and oceans during the *Mesozoic era*.

predator An animal that hunts other animals for food.

prehistoric animal An animal living before people existed.

prey An animal that is hunted by other animals for food.

pterosaurs Flying *reptiles* that lived during the *Mesozoic era*.

reptile A group of animals with scaly, waterproof skin, such as snakes and dinosaurs.

saurischian One of the two main groups of dinosaurs. Saurischian dinosaurs had hips shaped like lizards' hips.

sauropods A group of related plant-eating dinosaurs with long necks and long tails, such as Apatosaurus.

scavenge To look for animals that have already died, to eat as food, instead of hunting live *prey*.

sedimentary rock Rock made from sediment, such as sand or mud.

species (plural: species) A type of animal or plant. Males and females of the same species can breed, or have babies, with each other.

theropods A group of meat-eating *saurischian* dinosaurs that walked on two legs.

trace fossil The fossilized track or shape left behind by an animal or plant.

Triassic period A period of time 240–208 million years ago. The very first dinosaurs lived during the late Triassic period.

Internet links ....

Throughout this book we have recommended websites where you can find out more about dinosaurs. To visit the sites, go to the **Usborne Quicklinks Website** where you will find links to all the sites.

1. Go to **www.usborne-quicklinks.com**
2. Type the keywords for this book:
   discovery dinosaurs
3. Type the page number of the link you want to visit.
4. Click on the link to go to the recommended site.

Here are some of the things you can do on the websites recommended in this book:
- Watch video clips of dinosaurs.
- Build a dinosaur online.
- Play a game about fossils.
- Test your dinosaur knowledge with online quizzes.

Site availability

The links in Usborne Quicklinks are regularly reviewed and updated, but occasionally you may get a message that a site is unavailable. This might be temporary, so try again later, or even the next day. Websites do occasionally close down and when this happens, we will replace them with new links in Usborne Quicklinks. Sometimes we add extra links too, if we think they are useful. So when you visit Usborne Quicklinks, the links may be slightly different from those described in your book.

Downloadable pictures

Pictures marked with a ★ in this book can be downloaded from the Usborne Quicklinks Website. These pictures are for personal use only and must not be used for commercial purposes.

COMPUTER NOT ESSENTIAL
If you don't have access to the internet, don't worry. This book is a fun and informative introduction to dinosaurs.

Safety on the internet

Ask your parent's or guardian's permission before you connect to the internet and make sure you follow these simple rules:

- Never give out information about yourself, such as your real name, address, phone number or the name of your school.
- If a site asks you to log in or register by typing your name or email address, ask permission from an adult first.

What you need

To visit the websites you need a computer with an internet connection and a web browser (the software that lets you look at information from the internet). Some sites need extra programs (plug-ins) to play sound or show videos or animations.

If you go to a site and do not have the necessary plug-in, a message will come up on the screen. There is usually a link to click on to download the plug-in. For more information about plug-ins, go to Usborne Quicklinks and click on "Net Help".

Notes for parents and guardians

The websites described in this book are regularly reviewed, but the content of a website may change at any time and Usborne Publishing is not responsible for the content on any website other than its own.

We recommend that children are supervised while on the internet, that they do not use internet chat rooms, and that you use internet filtering software to block unsuitable material. Please ensure that your children read and follow the safety guidelines printed above. For more information, see the Net Help area on the Usborne Quicklinks Website.

Index

Page numbers in *italic* show where to find pictures. Where there are several pages for a particular entry, numbers in **bold** tell you where to find the main explanation.

Acknowledgements ....

Every effort has been made to trace the copyright holders of the material in this book. If any rights have been omitted, the publishers offer to rectify this in any subsequent editions following notification. The publishers are grateful to the following organizations and individuals for their permission to reproduce material (t=top, m=middle, b=bottom, l=left, r=right):

Cover © Joe Tucciarone/Science photo library; © Tetsuo Kushii (back cover artwork); **p1** © Horizon Originals and Chris Darga used by permission, all rights reserved, Jim Zuckerman/CORBIS; **p2-3** © Jonathan Blair/CORBIS; **p4-5** © The Natural History Museum, London, (background) © Digital Vision; **p5** © Chris Mattison; **p6-7** © Robert Holmes/CORBIS; **p7** (br) © Tom Bean/CORBIS; **p8** © Jonathan Blair/CORBIS; **p9** © The Natural History Museum, London; **p10-11** © Paul A. Souders/CORBIS, taken at the Royal Tyrrell Museum of Palaeontology, Alberta, Canada; **p11** © Horizon Originals and Chris Darga used by permission, all rights reserved; **p14-15** © The Natural History Museum, London; **p14** (bl) © The Natural History Museum, London; **p15** (br) © The Huntarian Museum, University of Glasgow; **p16** © The Natural History Museum, London; **p17** (background) © Digital Vision, (main) © Jonathan Blair/CORBIS; **p18** (tr) © François Gohier/Ardea London, (bl) © The Natural History Museum, London; **p19** (background) © Digital Vision, (main) © Horizon Originals and Chris Darga used by permission, all rights reserved; **p20-21** (background) © John Russell; **p20** © Horizon Originals and Chris Darga used by permission, all rights reserved; **p21** © The Natural History Museum, London; **p22** (bl) © The Natural History Museum, London; **p23** (tr) and (br) © The Natural History Museum, London; **p25** (background) © Digital Vision, (main) © J. Eastcott and Y. Momatiuk/Planet Earth Pictures; **p26-27** © The Natural History Museum, London; **p27** © Horizon Originals and Chris Darga used by permission, all rights reserved; **p28** (br) © Peter Smithers/CORBIS; **p30** (tl) © P. Morris/Ardea London, (b) © The Natural History Museum, London; **p31** (tl) and (br) © The Natural History Museum, London; **p32-33** © The Natural History Museum, London; **p34-35** (background) © Digital Vision; **p34** © The Natural History Museum, London; **p35** © Horizon Originals and Chris Darga used by permission, all rights reserved, Jim Zuckerman/CORBIS; **p36-37** © Horizon Originals and Chris Darga used by permission, all rights reserved; **p40** © Horizon Originals and Chris Darga used by permission, all rights reserved; **p41** © The Natural History Museum, London; **p42** © J. Eastcott and Y. Momatiuk/Planet Earth Pictures; **p47** © The Natural History Museum, London; **p48** © James A. Sugar/CORBIS; **p49** (tr) Don Davis/NASA, (b) © D. J. Roddy, U.S. Geological Survey; **p50-51** © Professor K. Seddon and Dr. T. Evans, Queens University, Belfast/Science Photo Library, (background) © Horizon Originals and Chris Darga used by permission, all rights reserved; **p50** © Layne Kennedy/CORBIS; **p52-53** © The Natural History Museum, London; **p54-55** (background) © Digital Vision; **p55** 1998 Slott, Fleming and Burnham used by permission, all rights reserved; **p56-57** (background) © Digital Vision; **p58** © Horizon Originals and Chris Darga used by permission, all rights reserved; **p59** © The Natural History Museum, London

Series editor: Gillian Doherty; Managing editor: Jane Chisholm; Managing designer: Mary Cartwright
Photographic manipulation: John Russell; Cover design: Zoe Wray